THE SECRET LIFE OF THE LOCH NESS MONSTER

by Benjamin Harper

CAPSTONE PRESS
a capstone imprint

Published by Capstone Press, an imprint of Capstone
1710 Roe Crest Drive, North Mankato, Minnesota 56003
capstonepub.com

Library of Congress Cataloging-in-Publication Data
Names: Harper, Benjamin, author.
Title: The secret life of the Loch Ness monster / by Benjamin Harper.
Description: North Mankato, Minnesota : Capstone Press, [2023] | Series: The secret
lives of cryptids | Includes bibliographical references and index. | Audience: Ages
9-11 | Audience: Grades 4-6 | Summary: "Think you know all about the Loch Ness
Monster? Think again! This underwater cryptid has a secret life that may surprise
you. Does Nessie have family swimming nearby? Is the creature in the lake a long-
lost dinosaur, giant eel, or something else? Uncover these exciting facts and more
through entertaining photos and easy-to-read text that supports struggling readers
and engages monster fans alike"— Provided by publisher.
Identifiers: LCCN 2022041533 (print) | LCCN 2022041534 (ebook) | ISBN
9781669004172 (hardcover) | ISBN 9781669040453 (paperback) | ISBN
9781669004134 (pdf) | ISBN 9781669004158 (kindle edition)
Subjects: LCSH: Loch Ness monster—Juvenile literature.
Classification: LCC QL89.2.L6 H267 2023 (print) | LCC QL89.2.L6 (ebook) | DDC
001.944—dc23/eng/20220829
LC record available at https://lccn.loc.gov/2022041533
LC ebook record available at https://lccn.loc.gov/2022041534

Editorial Credits
Editor: Abby Huff; Designer: Heidi Thompson; Media Researcher: Jo Miller;
Production Specialist: Tori Abraham

Image Credits
Alamy: Chronicle, 24, PictureLux/The Hollywood Archive, 29; Getty Images:
Khadi Ganiev, 27, Vaara, 13; Newscom: Academy of Applied Science Boston
Massachusetts/Mirrorpix, 20, Danny Lawson/ZUMA Press, 21, VICTOR HABBICK
VISIONS/SCIENCE PHOTO LIBRARY, 9, 19; Science Source: CCI Archives, 5;
Shutterstock: apien, 28, Art studio G, Cover (Loch Ness), Daniel Eskridge, 10,
Kariakin Aleksandr, 7 (dinosaur silhouette), kelttt, 6, 7 (snowflakes), Lubomira08,
14, LynxVector, 22, Michael Rosskothen, 15, Nastya Smirnova RF, 23, NOOR RADYA
BINTI MD RADZI, 11, Picture Partners, 12, s_karau, 25, S-F, 17 (inset), Stefano
Zaccaria, 17, Sudowoodo, Cover (hat), Tshooter, 7 (Scotland silhouette)

Design Elements
Shutterstock: dhtgip, Kues

All internet sites appearing in back matter were available and accurate when this
book was sent to press.

TABLE OF CONTENTS

Words in **bold** are in the glossary.

MEET THE LOCH NESS MONSTER

Who's the most famous monster in the world? The **Loch** Ness Monster, that's who! The watery **cryptid** was first spotted almost 1,500 years ago. People have been talking about it ever since. Fans even gave it a nickname. Nessie! Get the full scoop on the beast's secret life.

FACT

Cryptids are animals that people say they have seen. But no one can prove the beasts are real.

TEST YOUR NESSIE SMARTS!

Think you know all about the

Loch Ness Monster? Let's find out!

1. Which country does Nessie live in?

2. How long is Nessie?

3. When was the nickname Nessie

   first used?

4. What color is Nessie?

5. Does Nessie like warm water or cold?

ANSWERS

1. Scotland

2. Around 25 feet

3. 1940s

4. Gray, dark brown, or black

5. Cold

SWIMMING INTO THE SPOTLIGHT

Back in 564, Irish priest Columba was the first to meet Nessie. He wanted to cross the loch. A huge beast suddenly splashed up. Columba yelled at it to go away! It dove under the waves. Was it a monster attack? Or was Nessie saying hello?

FACT

No one knows if Nessie is male or female. People often call the cryptid *she* because of the nickname.

Nessie did stay away. Then in 1933, a couple was driving by the loch. A big gray animal crossed the road. It slid into the water. Newspapers reported the sighting. Soon, more people started seeing the cryptid. Nessie fever was born!

FACT

In Scottish Gaelic, the monster's name is Niseag. It's pronounced *NEE-shak.*

WHAT'S IN THE WATER?

Just what is the Loch Ness Monster? Eels live in the loch. Some people think Nessie might be a giant one. **Witnesses** have seen large humps in the water. Others say she's a big fish. Reports say she's around 25 feet long.

A regular eel is just as cool as a giant one. Right?!

BLAST FROM THE PAST

Could Nessie be related to dinosaurs? Based on sightings, many people think so. Long neck? Check! Flippers? Check!

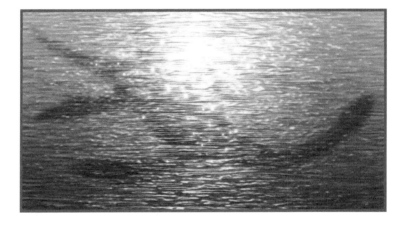

People say Nessie looks like a **plesiosaur**. These animals lived in oceans millions of years ago. Some think they got stuck in lakes as the earth shifted.

FACT

Di-NO-saur? A 2019 study didn't find any plesiosaur **DNA** in the loch's water.

HOME SWEET HOME

Nessie calls Scotland home. The closest city to her loch is Inverness. People there love having Nessie as a neighbor. They like to tell visitors about her!

MONSTER FAMILY

Scotland is also home to less famous lake monsters. Morag lives in Loch Morar. Lizzie swims in Loch Lochy. You might see Wee Oichy in Loch Oich.

Loch Ness

Inverness

A LOVELY LOCH

Nessie doesn't need the beach. She has Loch Ness! The chilly water is full of dead plant matter. It's the perfect hiding place.

LOCH NESS NUMBERS

 Loch Ness is 23 miles long.

 Loch Ness is 755 feet deep. That's longer than two Statues of Liberty on top of each other.

 Urquhart Castle sits on the shore. It was built in the 1200s.

SEARCHING FOR NESSIE

The hunt for Nessie is on! Scientists have led major searches over the past 100 years. They've searched with submarines. They've looked with **sonar** too. In 1972, scientists took underwater photos. Some say the pics show flippers. Was Nessie waving to the camera?

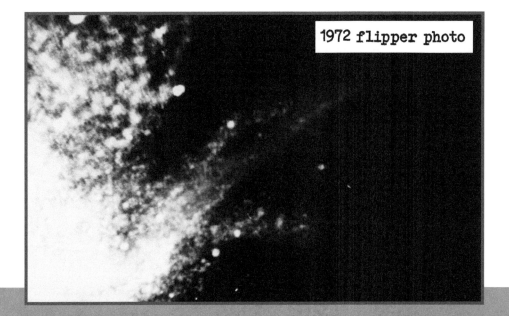

1972 flipper photo

FOOLED?

People have reported more than 1,100 Nessie sightings. Are they all the real deal? In 1933, a man said he found tracks made by Nessie. **Experts** checked them. Turns out, they were hippo prints. Someone made them using a stuffed hippo's foot.

In 1934, doctor Robert Kenneth Wilson snapped a pic. It showed a long neck sticking out of the loch. The "surgeon's photograph" became famous. The world saw Nessie!

LOCH NESS "MONSTER."

Or did it? In 1994, a person who helped

take the picture said it was faked.

TOTALLY FAMOUS!

Loch Ness is a **tourist** hot spot. Hundreds of thousands of people visit each year. They hope to get a peek of the watery cryptid. Brave fans can even take boat tours. They go out into the middle of Nessie's home.

Would you go on a boat in search of the monster?

FACT

A man lives in a van by the loch. He's been there for 30 years trying to get proof Nessie is real.

SCREEN SUPERSTAR

Can't go to Scotland, but want to know Nessie better? Check her out on screen! TV specials show the searches of Loch Ness. Nessie is also a movie star. She's in *Scooby-Doo and the Loch Ness Monster*, *The Water Horse*, and more.

What do you think? Is the Loch Ness Monster fact or fiction?

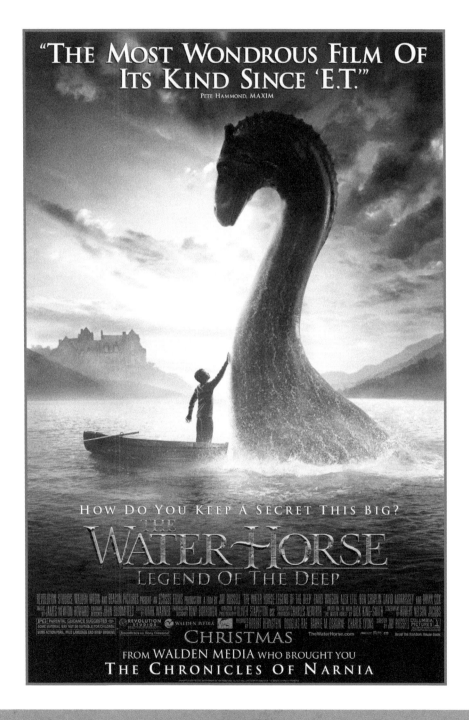

GLOSSARY

cryptid (KRYP-tid)—an animal that has not been proven to be real by science

DNA—material in cells that gives a living thing its own characteristics

expert (EK-spurt)—a person who knows a lot about a subject

loch (LAHK)—the Scottish word for lake

plesiosaur (PLEE-see-uh-sohr)—a large swimming reptile that lived during the time of the dinosaurs and had flippers and a long, snakelike neck

sonar (SOH-nar)—a device that uses sound waves to find underwater objects

tourist (TOOR-ist)—a person who travels to places for fun and to learn about them

witness (WIT-niss)—a person who has seen or heard something

READ MORE

Peabody, Erin. *The Loch Ness Monster.* New York: Little Bee Books, 2017.

Ransom, Candice. *Mysterious Loch Ness Monster.* Minneapolis: Lerner Publications, 2021.

Vale, Jenna and Martin Delrio. *Tracking the Loch Ness Monster.* New York: Rosen Publishing, 2018.

INTERNET SITES

Kiddle: Loch Ness Monster Facts for Kids
kids.kiddle.co/Loch_Ness_Monster

PBS: Unlocking the Mystery of Loch Ness
pbs.org/video/unlocking-the-mystery-of-loch-ness-kvfptc

Wonderopolis: Is the Loch Ness Monster Real?
wonderopolis.org/wonder/is-the-loch-ness-monster-real

INDEX

ABOUT THE AUTHOR

Benjamin Harper lives in Los Angeles where he edits superhero books for a living. When he's not at work, he writes; watches monster movies; and hangs out with cats Marjorie and Jerry, a betta fish named Toby, and tanks full of rough-skinned and eastern newts.